1 Straight Lines

To parents
Write your child's name and the date in the boxes. This exercise teaches your child how to draw straight lines. It is okay if he or she draws outside the path. Do the exercise along with your child if he or she has difficulty.

Name

Date

W9-BJJ-564

■ Draw a line from one picture to the matching picture.

Draw a line from one picture to the matching picture.

2 Straight Lines

■ Draw a line from one picture to the matching picture.

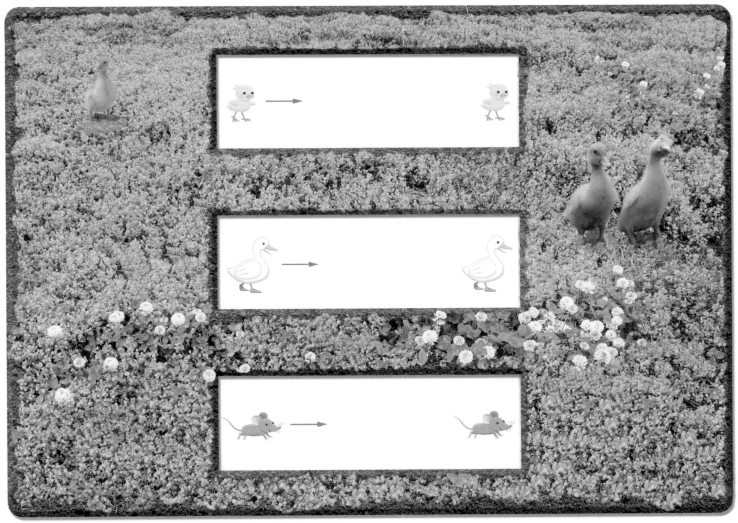

■ Draw a line from one picture to the matching picture.

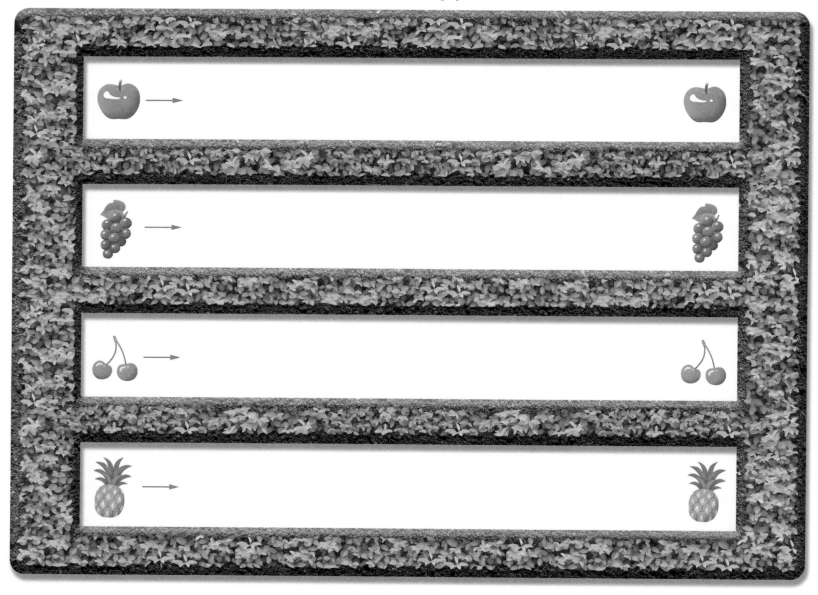

3 Straight Lines

Name

Date

■ Draw a line from one picture to the matching picture.

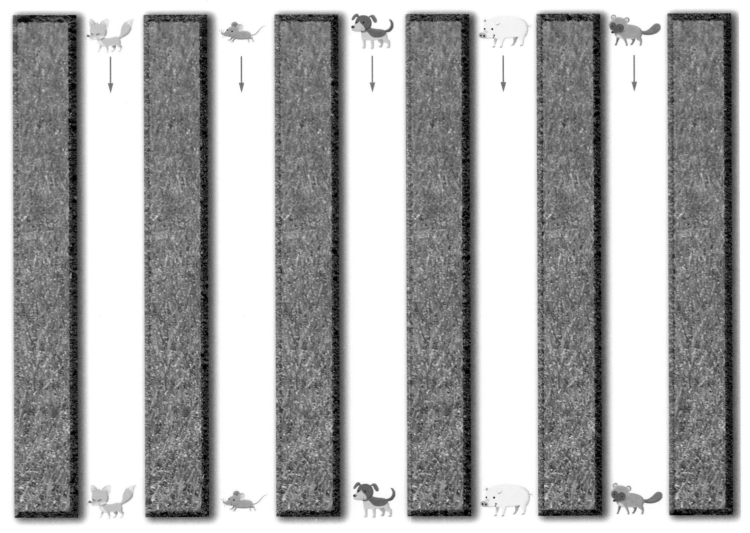

5

Draw a line from one picture to the matching picture.

4 Diagonal Lines

■ Draw a line from one picture to the matching picture.

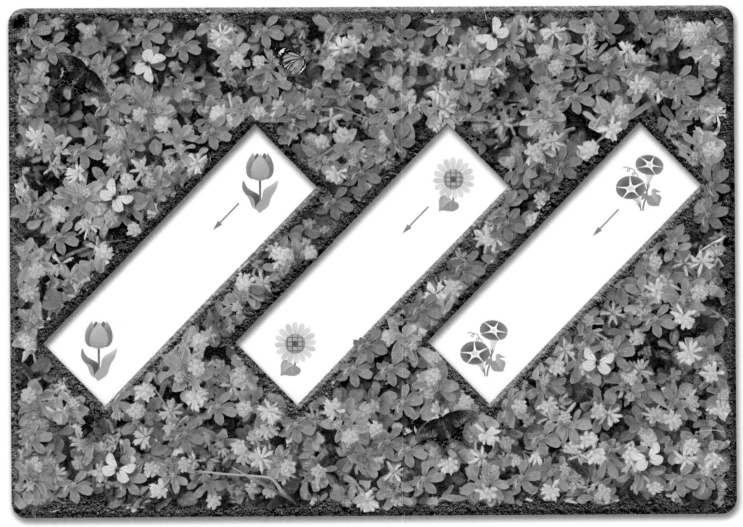

Name

Date

■ Draw a line from one picture to the matching picture.

5 Diagonal Lines

Name

Date

■ Draw a line from one picture to the matching picture.

■ Draw a line from one picture to the matching picture.

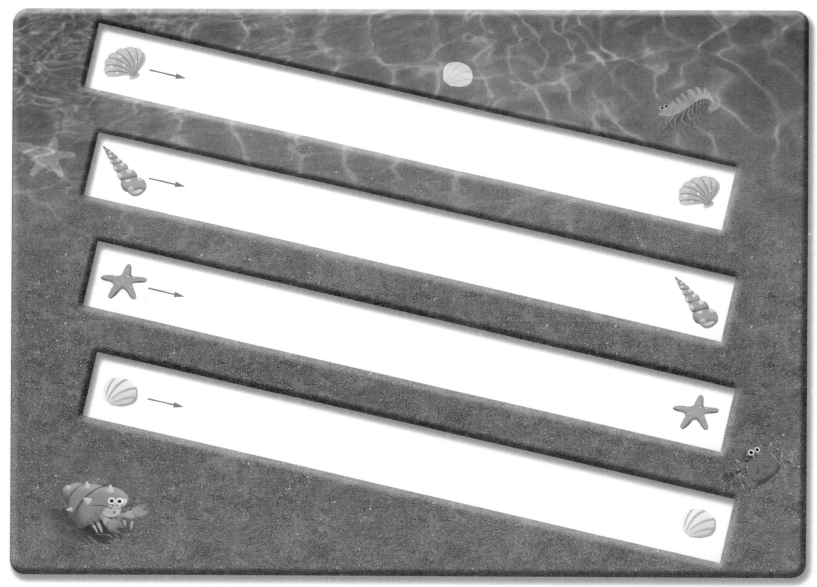

Diagonal Lines

■ Draw a line from one picture to the matching picture.

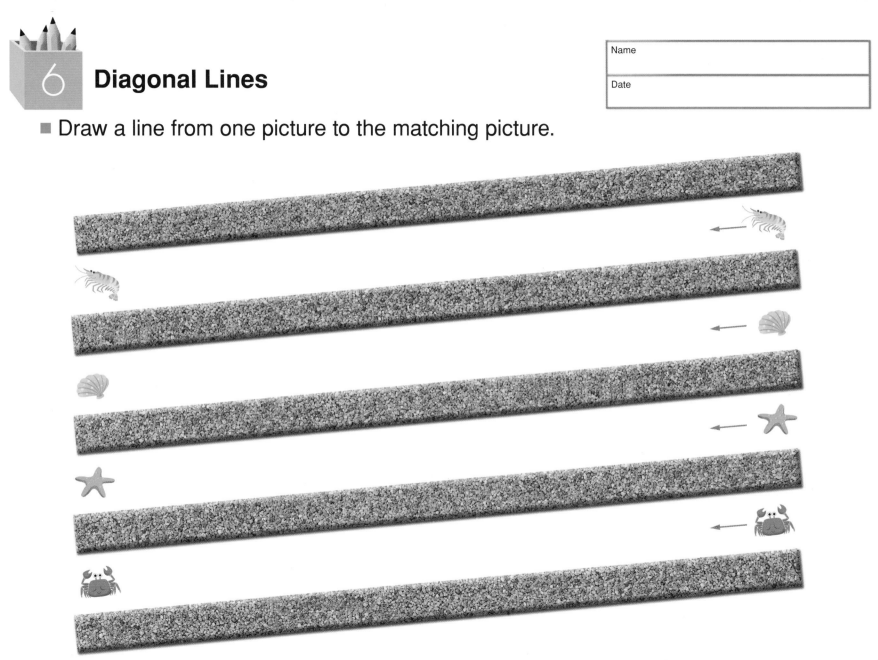

■ Draw a line from one picture to the matching picture.

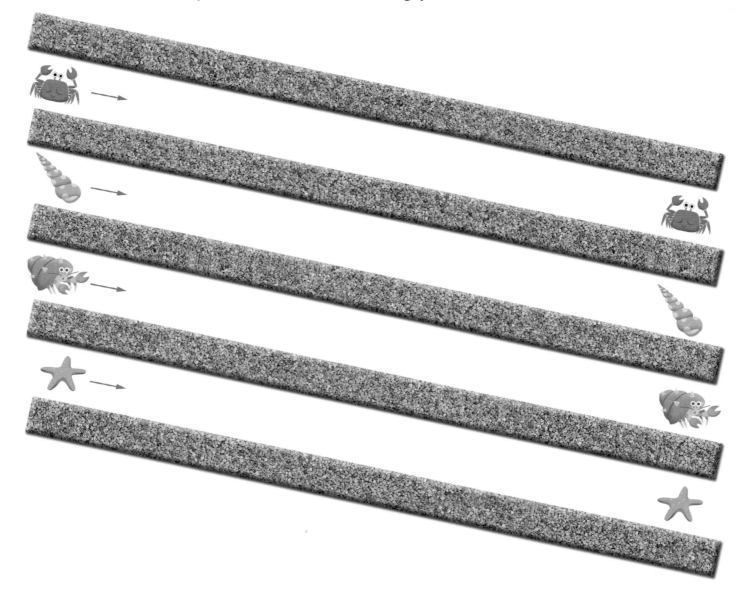

7 Jagged Lines

To parents
To make this activity easier, your child can complete each line using multiple strokes. Please encourage your child to draw a straight line to the middle arrow and then draw another straight line to the bottom.

Name

Date

■ Draw a line from one picture to the matching picture.

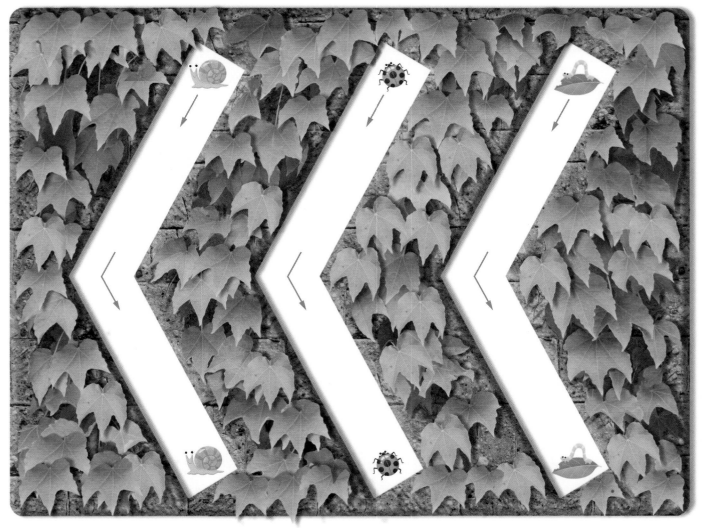

13

■ Draw a line from one picture to the matching picture.

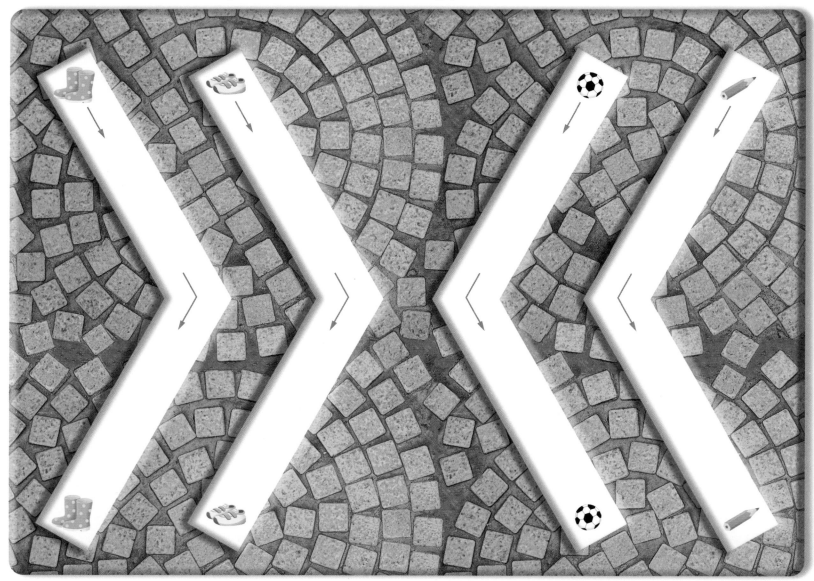

8 Jagged Lines

- Draw a line from one picture to the matching picture.

15

■ Draw a line from one picture to the matching picture.

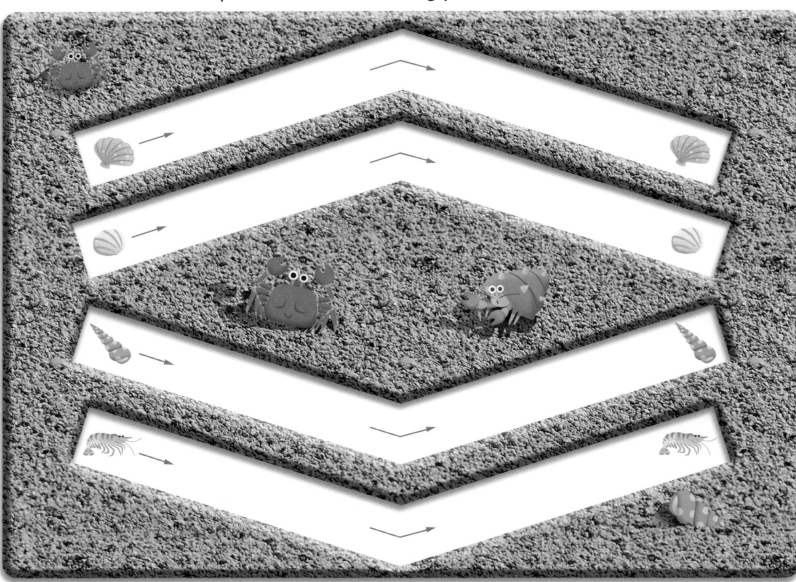

16

9 Curved Lines

To parents
This exercise teaches your child how to draw curved lines. Encourage your child to move his or her pencil slowly along the curved path.

Name

Date

■ Draw a line from the ● to the ★.

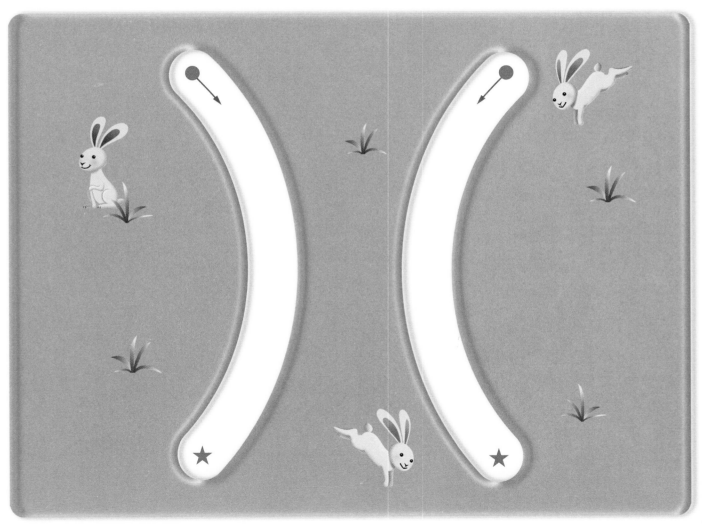

■ Draw a line from the ● to the ★.

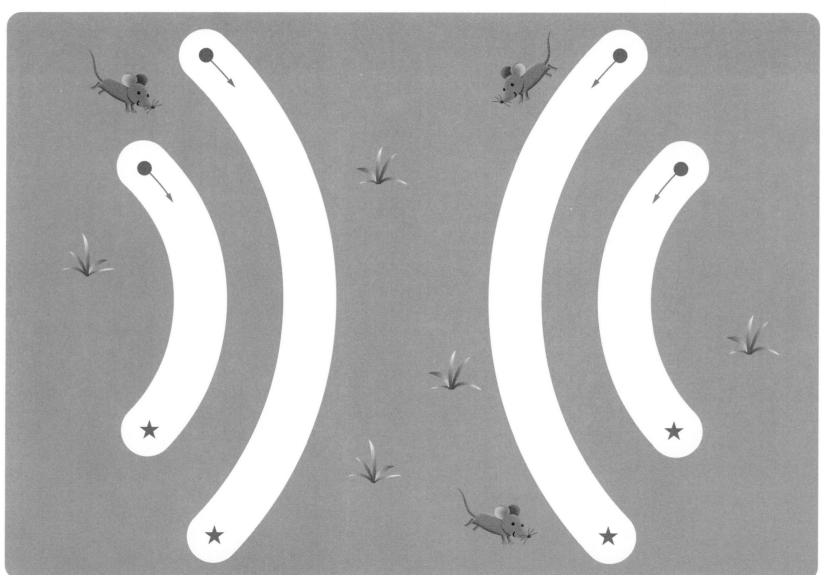

18

10 Curved Lines

■ Draw a line from the ● to the ★.

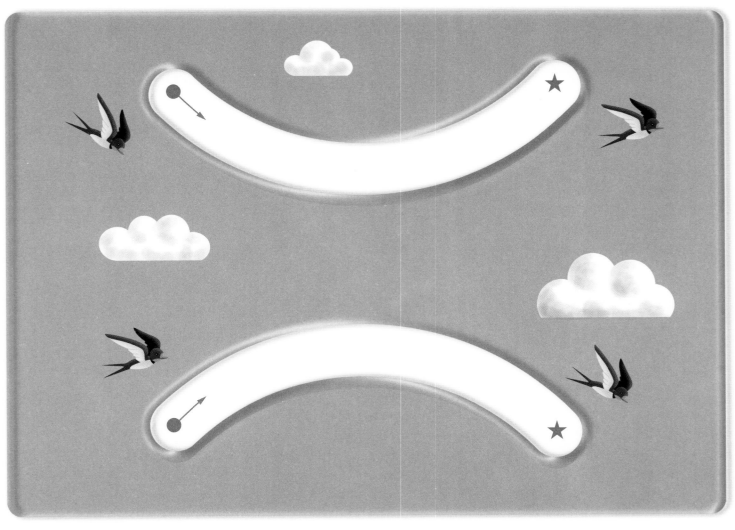

■ Draw a line from the ● to the ★.

20

11 Wavy Lines

■ Draw a line from the ● to the ★.

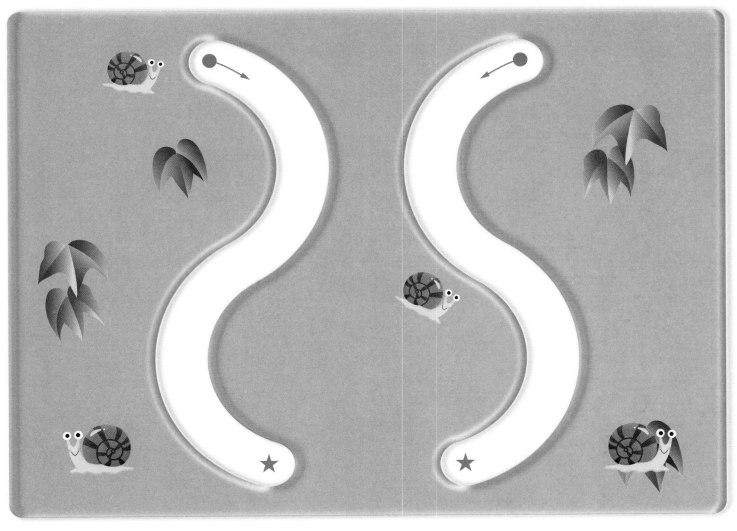

■ Draw a line from the ● to the ★.

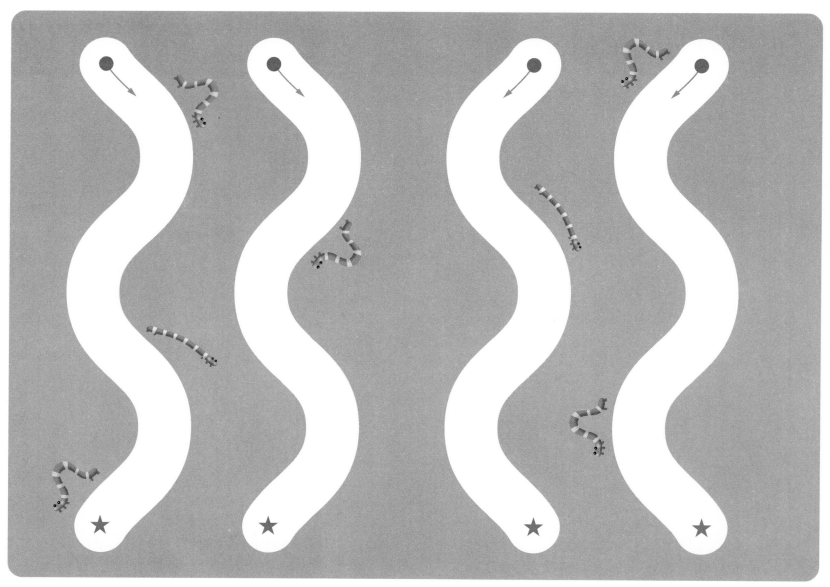

Wavy Lines

Name

Date

■ Draw a line from the ● to the ★.

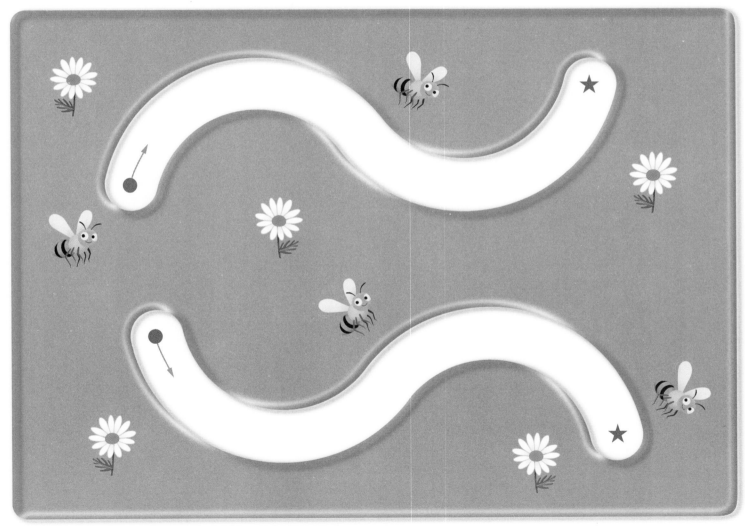

■ Draw a line from the ● to the ★.

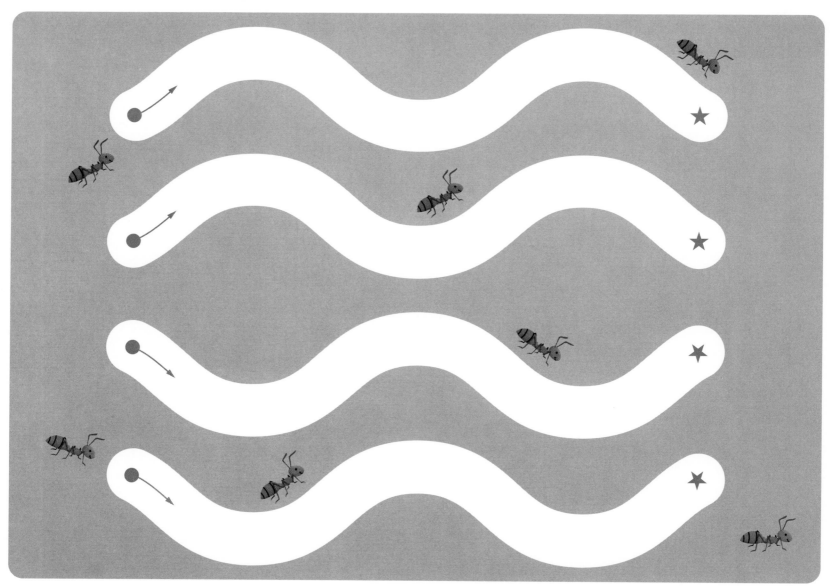

13 Zigzag Lines

Name

Date

■ Draw a line from the ● to the ★.

■ Draw a line from the ● to the ★.

Zigzag Lines

■ Draw a line from the ● to the ★.

■ Draw a line from the ● to the ★.

28

15 Circular Lines

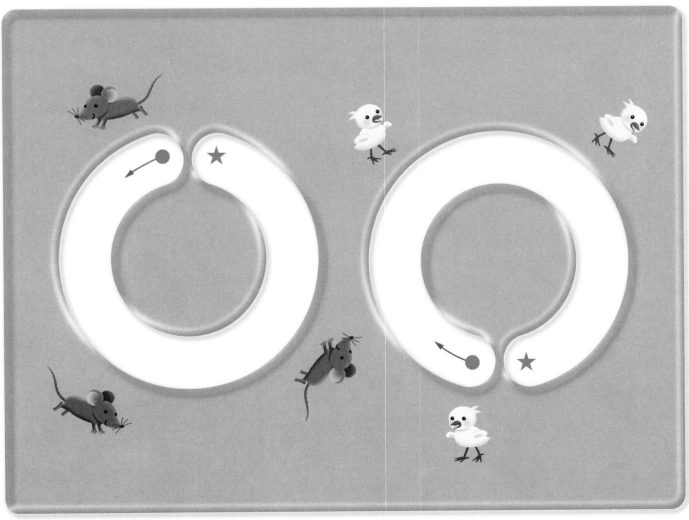

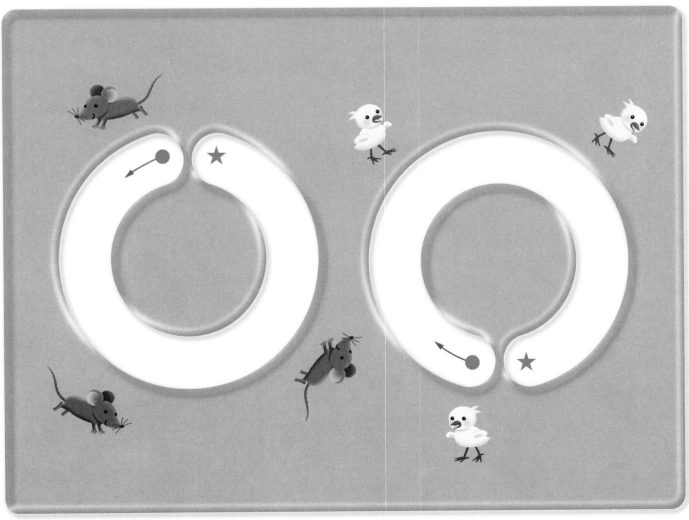

15 **Circular Lines**

15 **Circular Lines**

To parents
This exercise teaches your child how to draw circular lines. Encourage your child to move his or her pencil slowly along the curved path.

Name

Date

■ Draw a line from the ● to the ★.

■ Draw a line from the ● to the ★.

16 Circular Lines

Draw a line from the ● to the ★.

■ Draw a line from the ● to the ★.

17 Spiral Lines

■ Draw a line from the ● to the ★.

■ Draw a line from the ● to the ★.

18 Curved Lines

■ Draw a line from the ● to the ★.

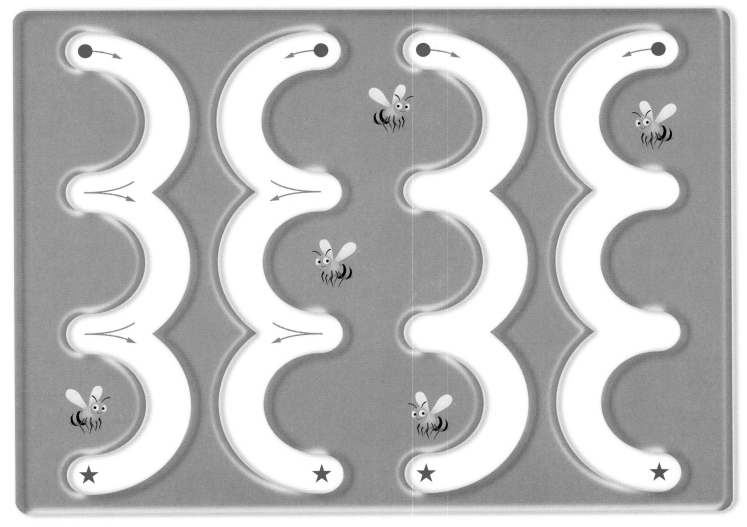

■ Draw a line from the ● to the ★.

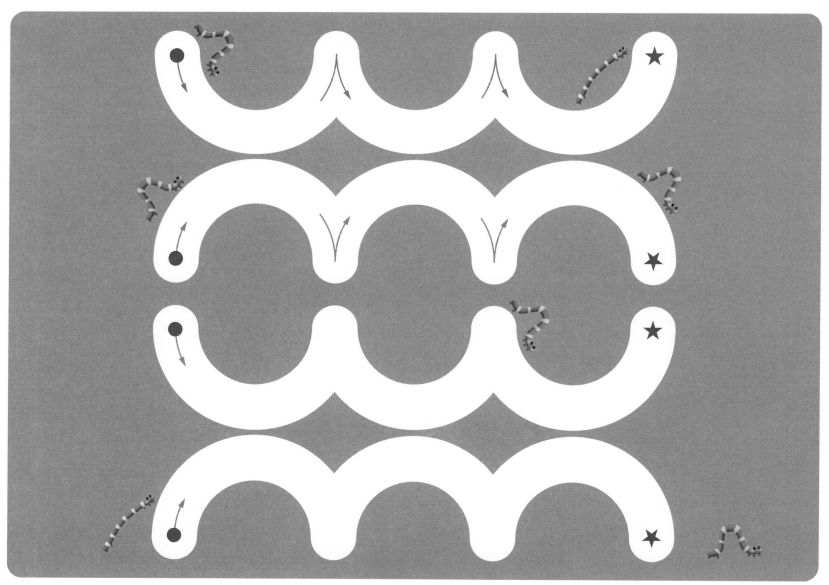

Lines That Loop

To parents
Make sure your child follows the arrows at the crossover points so that he or she draws in the correct direction.

Name

Date

■ Draw a line from the ● to the ★.

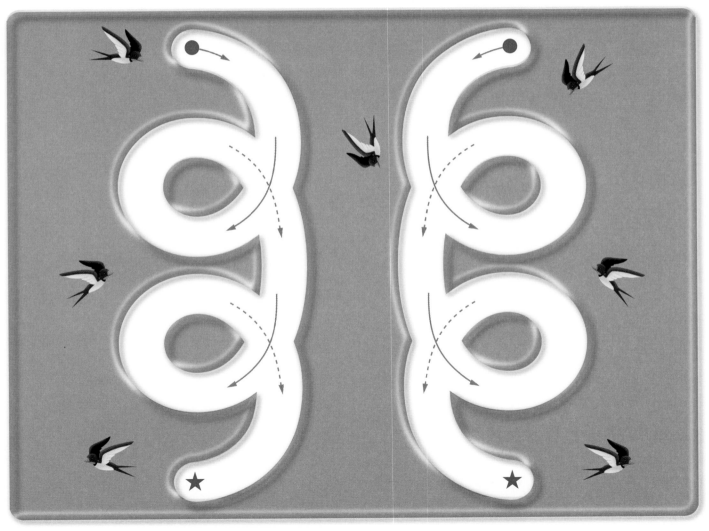

37

■ Draw a line from the ● to the ★.

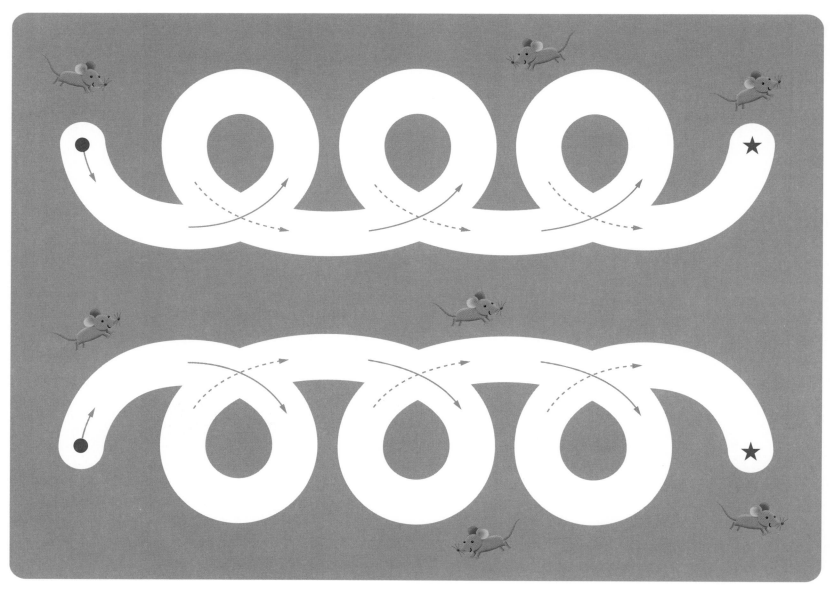

38

20 Long Lines

To parents

On the following pages, your child will encounter more comprehensive activities for drawing several kinds of lines. Encourage your child to have fun while drawing lines.

Name

Date

■ Draw a line from the ● to the ★.

Shoe

■ Draw a line from the ● to the ★.

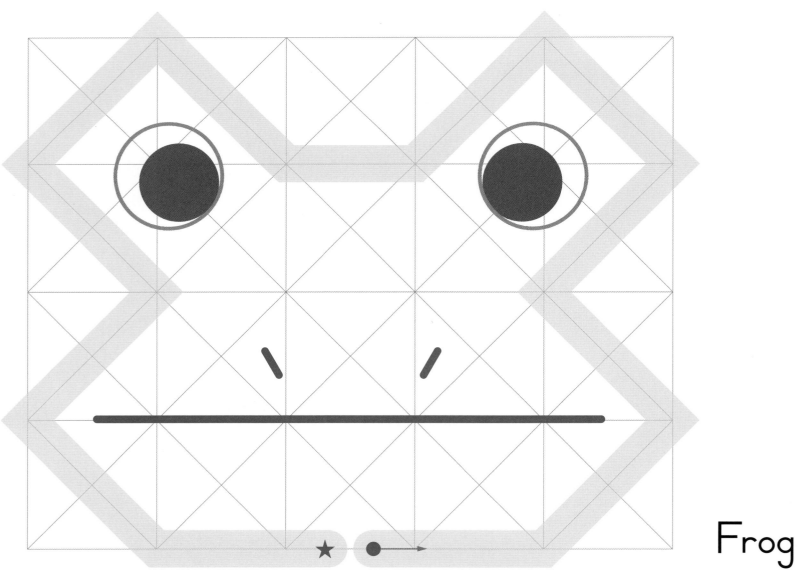

Frog

Long Lines

■ Draw a line from the ● to the ★.

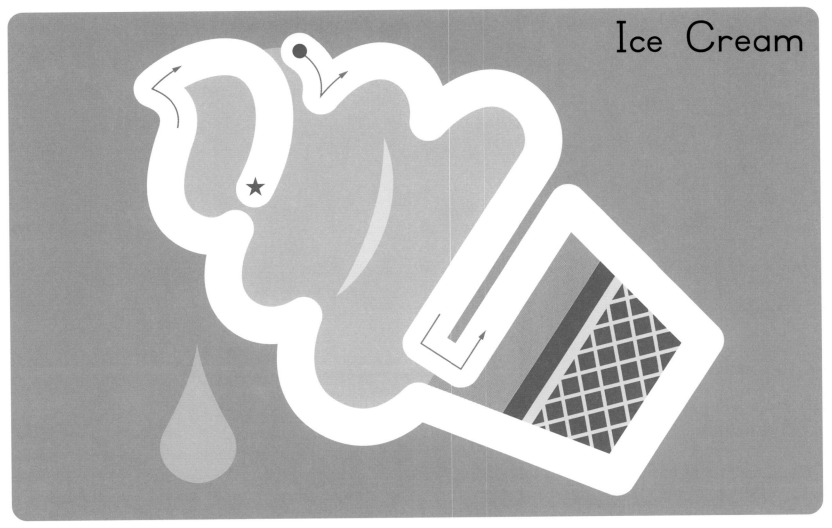

Ice Cream

Draw a line from the ● to the ★.

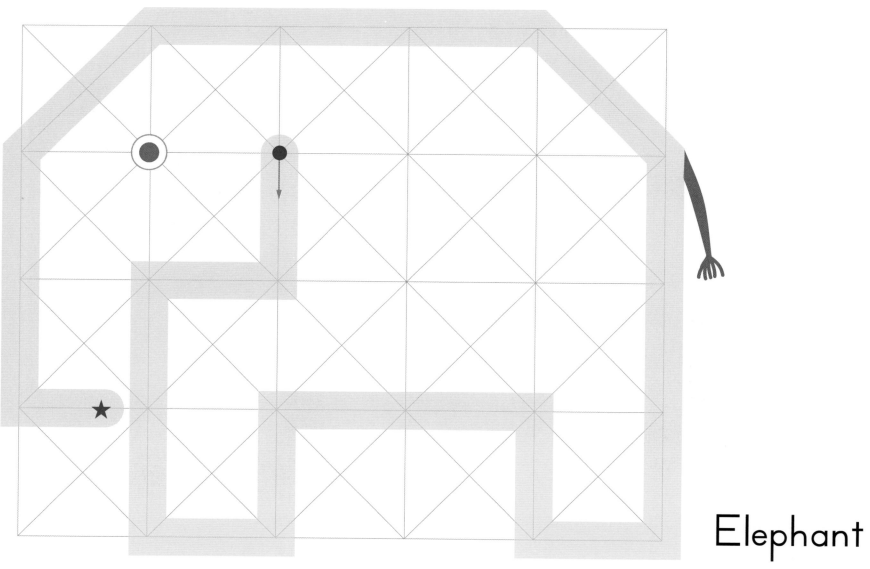

Elephant

22 Long Lines

■ Draw a line from the ● to the ★.

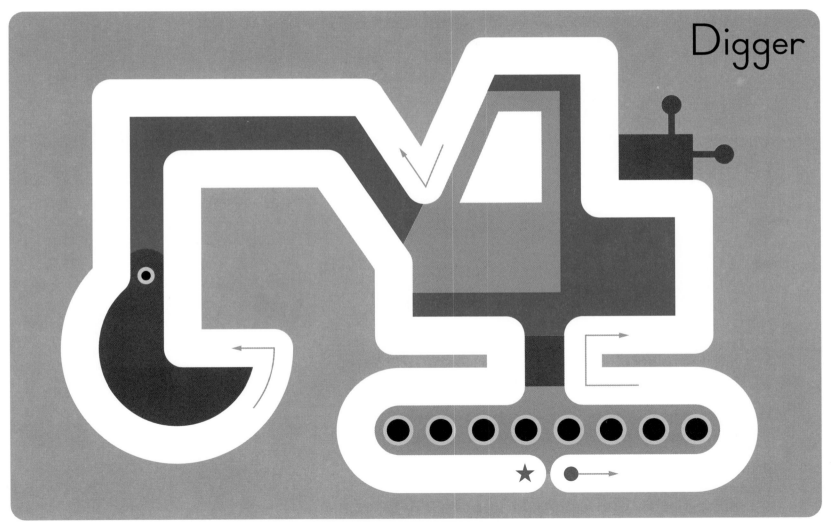

Digger

■ Draw a line from the ● to the ★.

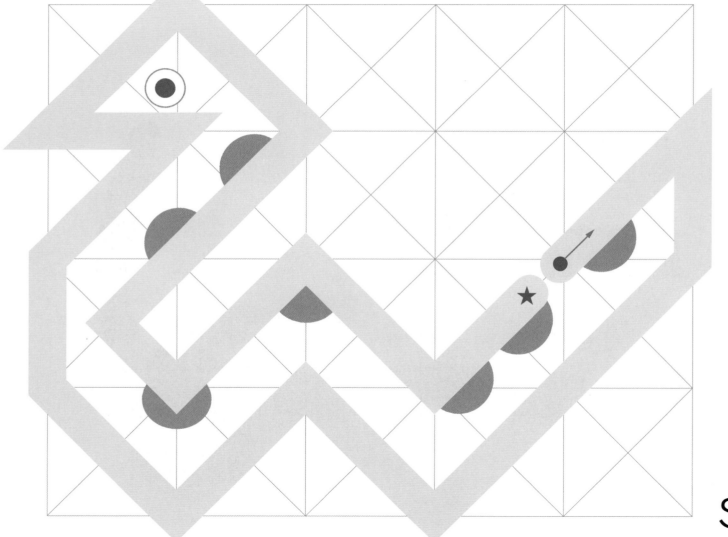

Snake

44

Long Lines

■ Draw a line from the ● to the ★.

Cat

■ Draw a line from the ● to the ★.

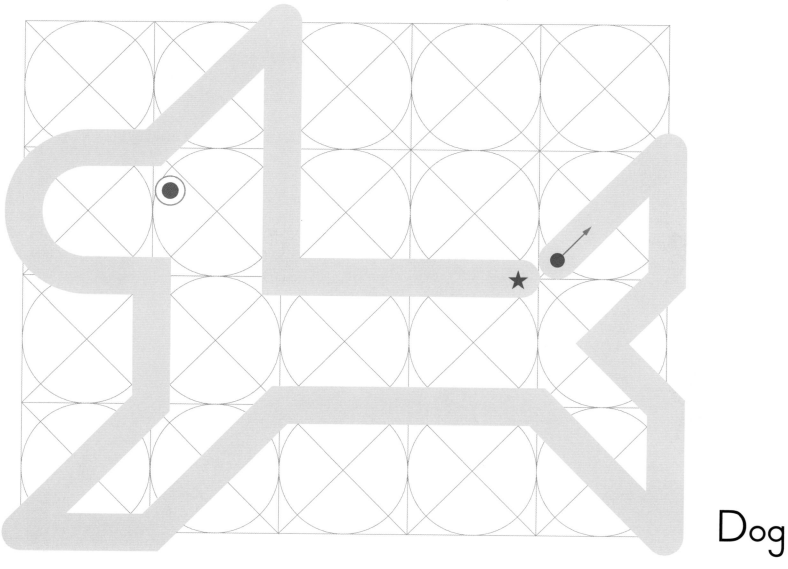

Dog

24 Long Lines

■ Draw a line from the ● to the ★.

Name	
Date	

Doll

47

■ Draw a line from the ● to the ★.

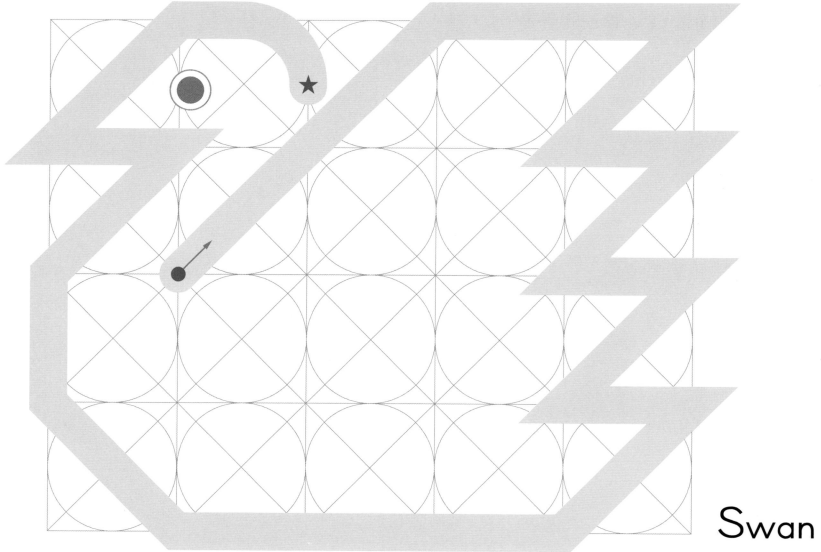

Swan

25 Long Lines

To parents
If your child has difficulty with this exercise, model the correct route by tracing the path with your finger. Encourage your child to move his or her pencil slowly along the curved path.

Name

Date

■ Draw a line from the ● to the ★.

■ Draw a line from the ● to the ★.

26 Long Lines

■ Draw a line from the ● to the ★.

51

■ Draw a line from the ● to the ★.

27 Long Lines

Name

Date

■ Draw a line from the ● to the ★.

■ Draw a line from the ● to the ★.

28 Long Lines

Name

Date

■ Draw a line from the ● to the ★.

■ Draw a line from the ● to the ★.

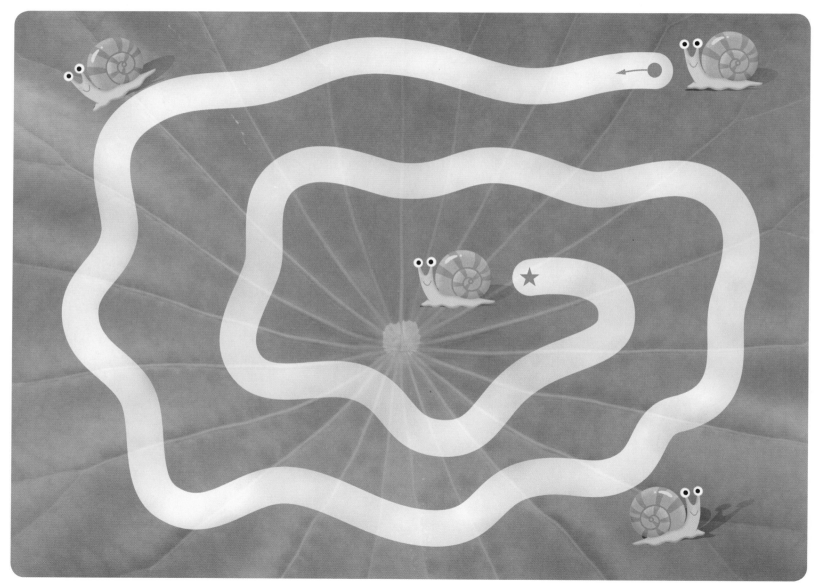

Long Lines

Draw a line from the ● to the ★.

■ Draw a line from the ● to the ★.

30 Long Lines

■ Draw a line from the ● to the ★.

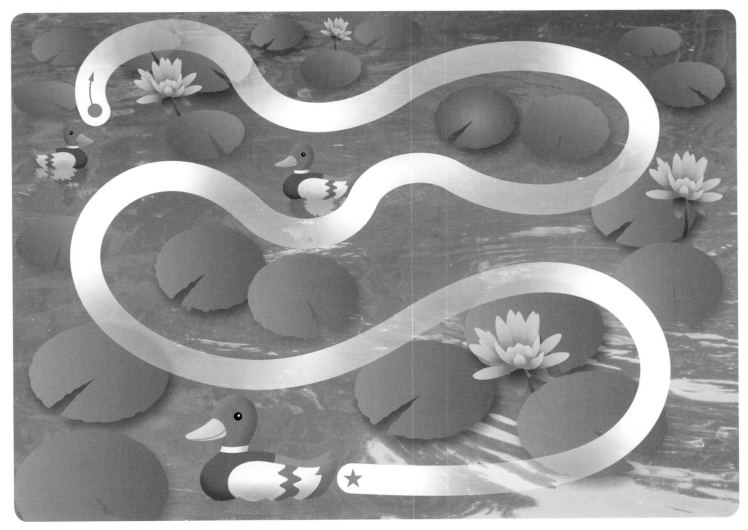

■ Draw a line from the ● to the ★.

31 Long Lines

Name

Date

■ Draw a line from the ● to the ★.

■ Draw a line from the ● to the ★.

32 Long Lines

■ Draw a line from the ● to the ★.

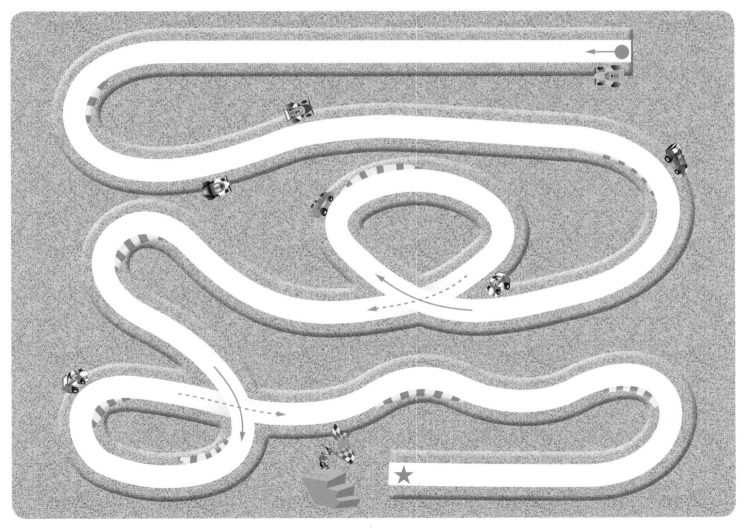

■ Draw a line from the ● to the ★.

To parents
We hope your child has had fun completing this workbook. By now he or she should be able to draw lines with more confidence and precision. Give your child lots of praise for his or her effort!